MIRACLE IN THE CARTON

BY

A N G E L S C E R E

Copyright © 2022 Angel Scere
All rights reserved
First Edition

Fulton Books
Meadville, PA

Published by Fulton Books 2022

ISBN 978-1-63860-929-2 (paperback)
ISBN 978-1-63860-930-8 (digital)

Printed in the United States of America

In loving memory of my beloved late grandmother,
Emily Quah, and my late father, Mr. Moses Scere.
To my beloved son, Terence Emmanuel Dickson,
my strength and hope to the Scere family.
To all who have inspired me along this journey
and every individual given birth by destiny.
To those who find life empty, aimless, and busy but not effective.
To those who will be reading this book, for
whom I desire a meaningful life characterized by
effectiveness, efficiency, and fulfillment.
To all who are oppressed by the ignorance of others.
To everyone that seeks hope and a strength for living.
To every dreamer out there who is still struggling
and fighting to accomplish their dreams.

CONTENTS

Acknowledgment vii
Introduction ix

Chapter 1: Unforgettable Experiences of My Village Life 1
Chapter 2: My Experience as a Refugee in Exile (Ivory Coast) 4
                Life in Côte d'Ivoire 4
                How I Met My Ex-Husband 6
                The Birth of My Son 8
Chapter 3: Visitation at Night 9
                The Appearance of My Late Father's Ghost
                in My Room at Night 11
                The Voice of God After the Death of My Father 11
                The Bible, the Green Comb, and the Dream 12
                The Dream 13
                The Meaning of the Dream 14
                What Is Forgiveness and What Is Not Forgiveness? .. 16
Chapter 4: The Agony of My Broken Marriage 19
Chapter 5: The Trauma of Abandonment 22
Chapter 6: Victim of Stigmatization 25
Chapter 7: God's Miracles Are Real 27
Chapter 8: I Put My Past Behind Me 33
                Guilt Causes Shame 37
                Guilt Can Diminish Self-Esteem 38
                Overcoming Guilt 39
                Seven Ways of Overcoming Your Past 40

Chapter 9:   I Did Overcome and Came Out of My
              Valley of Unbearable Experiences 42
Chapter 10: Creating a Future for Yourself 53
Chapter 11: Lessons Learned 56
              Practical Lessons to Learn about My
              Grandmother's Village Life 57
Chapter 12: My Achievements over the Years 62

ACKNOWLEDGMENT

Writing a book about the story of your life is harder than I thought. The entire experience was surreal from the outset. I must start by thanking the Almighty God for His bountiful blessings, especially for preserving my life amid all my challenges, giving me strength, and providing the resources for this project.

I am eternally grateful to my late grandmother, Ms. Emily Quah, who became the parent figure in my life and sustained me. She instilled so many good values in me that have helped me succeed in life.

To my beloved son, Terence Dickson, I thank you for your unflinching support.

A very special thanks to Mr. Mark McCauley for his advice and support. None of this would have been possible without you. It is because of your efforts and encouragement that I have a legacy to pass on to my family.

I am forever grateful to Mrs. Christine Sonpon Freeman for her editorial help and keen insight in bringing my story to life.

Thanks to Fulton Books, the publisher.

To Ms. Yolanda Mac, CEO of *Sapphire Emerald Magazine*, thank you for bringing me on as an employee and giving me the opportunity to rise and serve as the first brand ambassador for *Sapphire Emerald Magazine*, thereby exposing me to the world. Without the experience from this job and support from you and my coworkers, this book would not exist.

A special thanks to Mr. Robert Perham for believing in me and seeing something in me that I couldn't see.

To Angel Foundation Crew, I say thank you. You sustained me in ways that I never knew I needed.

To my family: my brothers, John and Cletus Scere, my uncles, Jonathan Scere and Alexander Blotey Scere, and sister, Patricia Nimley, thank you.

Finally, thanks to all those who have been a part of my getting there: Pastor Erasmus Jarkloh, my spiritual mother, Rebecca Holmes, and her beloved husband, Dixon Holmes, my spiritual father, Prophet Leo Mayson, and his prayer line, Solution Temple, Pastor Ernest Jerome Yancy and Mother Pauline Yancy of Blue Print International Church, and Lion of Judah Prayer Team. To my spiritual sisters: Catherine Dweh and sisters Bubu, Cece Jones, Agnes Zeh, and my goddaughter, Bella Zeh, I say thank you.

INTRODUCTION

Do you feel hopeless and confused and want to give up? Are you depressed because of the challenges that you are faced with? Are you experiencing a painful breakup? Have you experienced the trauma of parental abandonment? Do you need help in overcoming failures? This book will help you leave the pain and anger behind and move on with your life.

Whether you are suffering from a recent loss or a lingering wound from the past and whether you are in a relationship in which you no longer feel loved, as you read this book, you will find support to help yourself. You will learn that with faith and resilience, you can overcome any situation.

Abandoned by my mother, I was sent by my dad to a rural village in a developing country with unfavorable conditions to be raised by my grandmother, who had no money to support me. Our struggles were exacerbated by the Liberian Civil War, which started in December 1989. It was a harrowing experience, and we were compelled to flee the country for fear of being killed. My life in exile is another painful experience.

This book is written to give hope to the hopeless. To encourage people to stand firm and keep pressing forward no matter what may come their way. It is my hope that as you read this book, you will learn that life, after all, is worth living, and you will find a reason to move forward with your life.

CHAPTER 1

UNFORGETTABLE EXPERIENCES OF MY VILLAGE LIFE

I first became aware of myself in a village in Banwin, Maryland County, Republic of Liberia. I found myself living with my paternal grandmother. My mother had placed me in a carton and left it at my dad's apartment door even though he was not home when she arrived. A neighbor spotted the box at the door and peeped inside, curious to know why it was there. There I was, lying down with a bottle in my mouth. She wasted no time contacting my dad to inform him about what she had seen and inquired whether he was aware. Of course, he wasn't.

He quickly returned home and met me lying in the box at the entrance of his door and had to deal with the situation. Being a single man at the time and busy with work, he called his mother, my grandmother, to take me to live with her.

My grandmother and I lived in a house made of clay and palm thatch, found in most rural areas in Africa. It was an unconducive environment that lacked even the basic necessities. We had no bed, so we had to place our mat on the dirt floor to sleep.

Hygiene was a severe problem. We used the bush for the restroom as the hut lacked one. We used leaves to wipe ourselves whenever we went into the bush to attend to nature as we did not have toilet paper. We used clothes to absorb the menstrual discharge during the menstrual period since we did not have sanitary pads. The mosquitoes were our regular visitors, and we fell sick all the time from mosquito bites. This was one of the harshest periods of my life. Food was a real challenge for us. My grandmother had to struggle to get food, so she always cooked late. As a result, I went to bed many nights without eating. Can you imagine your kid being hungry all day and sleeping without eating because of late cooking? The entire village lacked electricity and safe drinking water. We used firewood to cook our food, as light to see at night, and keep warm since there was no electricity. We also had to go to the creek daily for water.

There was no local school that I could attend to improve myself. Therefore, I spent my days on the farm helping my grandmother. Because of the absence of my parents, she became a dominant influence in my life. She taught me to farm, work hard, be humble and the importance of teamwork. She also taught me how to build a relationship with God and pray without relying on a pastor, apply wisdom to things a person does, never allow age to limit my work, and that I should continue working as long as I have the strength.

Farming is a way of life for people in rural areas. It is an arduous task that requires teamwork. You will always see people working together in groups whenever you go to a farm. It was more of a career for my grandmother, who was passionate about it.

Whenever she was going to the farm, she always took me along to teach me. When the crops were ready, we would harvest and sell them.

Selling the harvested crops is something that I looked forward to. It brightened my childhood, and I have never forgotten that experience. My grandmother and I would go around the village and sometimes to town to sell coconut candy, rice bread, cassava, corn, pepper, etc. Typically, our selling of these commodities was done over the weekends, specifically Friday and Saturday. It started to annoy me and turned into a permanent irritant because I should have been in school.

Walking is a way of life for people living in rural areas, and we had to walk to and from the farm and any other place we had to go. There were times when I felt tired, and my grandmother would put me on her back to reach wherever we were going. This experience of my village life has taught me a lesson of adjustment to cultural norms. While struggling with abandonment, near starvation, and other unfavorable conditions associated with village life, my country Liberia was plunged into a civil war. People were being killed at the hands of soldiers and from stray bullets. Food was scarce, and people were afraid to find food for fear of being killed. Many heinous crimes were being committed, and it was scary not knowing who would be next. We, therefore, fled the country and went into exile in neighboring Côte d'Ivoire for refuge.

CHAPTER 2

MY EXPERIENCE AS A REFUGEE IN EXILE (IVORY COAST)

LIFE IN CÔTE D'IVOIRE

The Liberian Civil War between Charles Taylor and Samuel K. Doe, which started from 1989 to 1997, forced my grandmother and me into exile in Côte d'Ivoire, a neighboring country, as refugees. While on the Ivory Coast, we resided in a city called Tabou. We lived in a seven-bedroom house constructed by my uncles with materials similar to the one we had lived in Liberia. We prayed that it would not rain many days because we could not stay in the house when it did. After all, the palm leaves used for the roof could not keep the rain out. Whenever it did rain, the whole place was soaked, and we had to seek shelter elsewhere. We thought that going to the Ivory Coast was an opportunity to live a better life. Still, instead, it was from worse to ridiculous.

We partially survived on the crops we planted, supervised by my Uncle Jonathan. Every morning, my grandmother and I and some other relatives would go with Uncle Jonathan to grow cabbage, onions, tomatoes, watermelon, carrots, etc., in the garden. After planting the crops, we fertilize them to enable them to grow to our expectations. We usually worked in the garden from the morning hours to the afternoon.

When it was time to harvest, we would do so and take some of the crops to the market for sale. Whenever we went to sell, we would not return home before 6:30 p.m. Cooking would commence upon our return from the farm. It would be rather late by the time the food was ready, and I would have fallen asleep by then, hungry without eating anything. Even though we made the garden, it was not sufficient for us. So we would go to communities where wealthy people, like the Lebanese, resided to find canned food from their trash cans to augment what we had so that we would not die of starvation. We also used to get used clothes from them that they no longer wanted.

I was eager to improve myself. I enrolled in a French school because the English school at that time cost money, and my grandmother and uncle could not afford financially to send me to an English school. They could not even afford to buy me a book bag. I was constrained to put my books into a plastic bag for school. They also could not afford to buy me a pair of shoes. I wore an old pair of rubber slippers to school. The slippers were old to the extent that I had to use a diaper pin at the toe area to keep them on my feet. I had one uniform that was so old that I used to be embarrassed whenever I was among my friends at school.

As time went by, United Nations built an English school specifically for refugees. I quickly took advantage and started attending the school known as ADRA. My enrollment in the ADRA as a student was highly phenomenal. I was actively involved with almost all the activities of the school. I joined the school choir, the baseball team, the quizzing team, etc. ADRA was one of the schools offering quality education, and my enrollment there, as a young girl growing up, helped mold and build me academically, morally, and spiritually. ADRA Elementary and Junior High School were known for their discipline and restrictions. My being there as a student has helped me immensely in being who I am and where I am today.

As we lived on the Ivory Coast, my grandmother got sick. Her sickness was so profound that her flesh fell off her body. We had to put plastic on her bed to sleep on so that her skin would not stick to it. She became bedridden, and it made me very sad to see her in that condition. My mother, the strongest woman that I have ever known, was broken and lying in bed twenty-four hours a day, seven days a week, and four weeks a month without being able to do anything for herself. I was unable to support her financially and spiritually at the time, and it depressed me because she had been my backbone.

There was a nickname that we used to call grandmother, which is known as Sisi. Whenever I went to her room while she was sick, I used to call her by her nickname and say, "Sisi will not die, you will overcome your sickness." But unfortunately, in 1996, my grandmother died.

With the death of my grandmother, I felt frustrated and hopeless because she had been the only person there for me all my life. It was the beginning of several pains and afflictions in my life. Thoughts of how my parents had treated me began to return. But God, being faithful, sent someone to assist me.

A friend of my dad's, called Patricia, accepted me into her home. She treated me like her biological child by showing me the same kindness she showed to her biological children. There was no distinction, abuse, or ill-treatment of me. She treated everyone in the house the same. I lived with her until she decided to return home to Liberia.

HOW I MET MY EX-HUSBAND

He left Abidjan and went to Tabou to visit his parents. While in Tabou, our paths crossed, and we became friends. Upon his return to Abidjan, he sent for me to go to him, and things began to get brighter for me. He lived in a crowded house with other tenants, so he took me to the home of one of his female friends to live. I visited him from time to time. After a while, he took me from his friend's place. He carried me back to his house because some gentlemen were always coming to his friend's place for a visit, and he felt insecure because of jealousy. However, taking me back to the crowded house that he was in was difficult because I had to join the women there to work tirelessly to keep the house clean. I also joined them in cooking and putting food on the table. This lifestyle was hard for me because I was not used to it, but I had no option but to cope with it. Coping with it allowed me to learn a lot of things about family life and the maintenance of my home as a woman.

After a period, the Lord blessed my friend with a teaching job at an American international school. With the job, we could pay for a place of our own and move out of that house with so many tenants. Moreover, my son's father bought a taxi for the transportation business with the job. He also invested money into a communication business.

Everything turned out well for us to the point where we could assist people in our surroundings and not go to them for help. Some people were amazed at how things had turned around for us to be able to assist others. But then, that's how God works. He can lift you out of any situation. You just must trust Him. It is written, "Whoever believes on Him will not be put to shame" (Romans 10:11 NKJV).

In the year AD 2003, we were joined together in holy matrimony in Abidjan, Côte d'Ivoire. We lived there and struggled together in peace and harmony until the opportunity to travel to the United States of America was opened. Within a few years, after we arrived in the United States of America, God blessed us with a son.

THE BIRTH OF MY SON

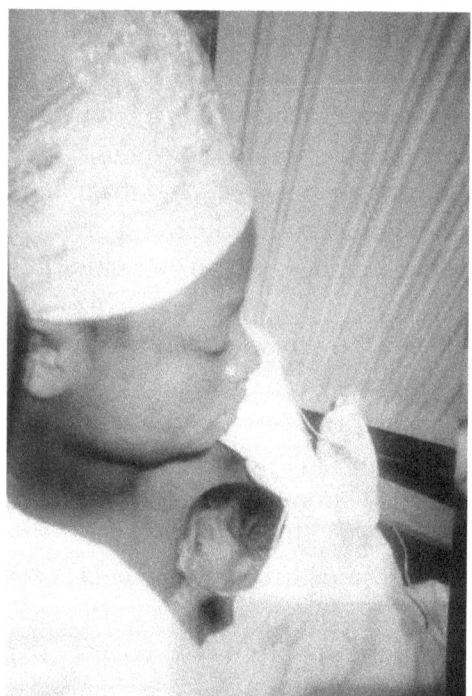

Amid a throng of nurses and doctors, my son Ted was born. I had been rushed to the hospital because I had developed complications while en route to visit a friend. It was a situation of one of us dying and the other living. Since it was not God's plan for us, we both survived.

Ted was born premature, three months before the due date, so his body and organs were not fully developed. Besides that, he had problems with his breathing. Every time he was scheduled to go home, he would stop breathing. So the doctors kept him there to diagnose his case. After a while, they advised that he undergo surgery at another hospital. He was transferred to the Cook Children's Medical Center, where the surgery was done. To God be the glory, it was successful. He stayed in the hospital for six months after his birth before he could finally go home.

CHAPTER 3

VISITATION AT NIGHT

In this chapter, my emphasis will be on unforgiveness because I have been a victim of unforgiveness related to my relationship with my biological father.

During the early part of my father's life as a young man, he was involved with several women who gave birth to fourteen children for him. Of the several girlfriends and young ladies with whom he had relationships, he got married to one of them, an African American woman. She had two kids for him, and it was these two kids that he was partially focused on as it relates to parental support as a father, neglecting the rest of his children.

My father's partial attitude in providing for us as his children created a serious conflict between him and me. Whenever I tried to discuss the issue with him, he got angry with me. Many days, one of us would hang up the phone on the other person. This conflict continued between us for a long period.

All I wanted from my dad was for him to realize his mistake and feel the pain that I felt—the pain of rejection and abandonment. But his ego would not permit him to feel my pain, and therefore, he would not apologize for his actions that caused so much pain and damage to my life as a child growing up. As a result, this conflict lasted for so long because he would not acknowledge his errors and apologize, and neither was I willing to just forgive him like that. At a certain point, we stopped communicating with each other on the phone because talking on the phone was like a war between him and me.

After a few months, I was led by the Holy Spirit to fast for three days. On the third day of the three days, my room door was opened at about 4:00 a.m. in the morning when I saw a shadow entering my room. This shadow was the ghost of my late father, but I did not know it at the time because I was not aware that he had died. When this happened, I was so scared that I quickly went into my bathroom and switched the light on. However, the light could not help me because I was overwhelmed by fear. After a few minutes, I got on my knees and began to pray. When I was done praying, I went back to bed. While sleeping, I had a dream, and in the dream, I heard a strange voice saying, "Call your father and tell him that you have forgiven him."

This voice was not the voice of the devil but the voice of God. The next morning, when I woke up, I called my dad's phone to tell him that I had forgiven him, but his phone rang for the longest without any response. I called his wife to find out what was happening to his phone, and to my utmost surprise, she said, "It was good that you called. Moses is dead." I fell to the floor, and darkness overtook me. I felt regret and guilt, and I was deeply troubled. I regretted and felt guilty for not forgiving my father when he was alive. The best time to forgive someone is when that person is still alive. On the other hand, the best time for someone to forgive you is when you are still alive. If someone does something evil to offend you, don't wait for that person to die before you forgive them.

On the other hand, if you did something wrong to hurt someone, don't wait for the person to die, then you go to their grave to ask for forgiveness. Forgive your husband, your wife, your children, your parents, your neighbors, etc., while they are still alive before it gets too late for you.

MIRACLE IN THE CARTON

The Appearance of My Late Father's Ghost in My Room at Night

After my father's death, it was in the night that his ghost appeared in my room. This is why I named this chapter "Visitation at Night." There is a reason why my father's ghost appeared to me after his death, and that reason was that he grieved for my forgiveness in his grave. And this is why his ghost appeared to me to awaken my consciousness to forgive him.

The Voice of God After the Death of My Father

After the death of my father, God spoke to me in my dream to forgive him because God himself had forgiven him while he was still alive. This simply means that refusing to forgive someone for hurting you does not, in any way, mean that God has not forgiven them. Your carrying grief and malice for someone in your heart does not mean that God in heaven is also carrying grief and malice in His heart for that person. No, my friend, do not be deceived into thinking that way.

You see, God, our heavenly father, is the God of forgiveness. Therefore, if somebody kills your mother or your father and that person asks you to forgive them. You refuse; when they sincerely ask God to forgive them for whatever they did to you, God can answer their prayers and forgive them because He is the God of mercy (1 John 1:9). And if you refuse to forgive someone for hurting you, that person sincerely asks God for forgiveness. God forgives them; that person is automatically free from the guilt and judgment of whatever they did to you. So if you are still harboring grief and malice in your heart for them, you are messing with yourself because they are free, and you are still locked up in the cave of unforgiveness.

I firmly believe that when my father was still alive, he asked God to forgive him for whatever pain he may have caused me, and God did forgive him. The fact that God forgave him made him automatically free from the guilt and the judgment of whatever pain he caused me. My father knew that I was not free based on my unforgiveness toward him. Therefore, when he died, his ghost appeared to me to awaken my consciousness to forgive him so that I could be free.

This corresponds with my dream after his death when God spoke to me to call him and tell him that I had forgiven him. Do you know what? Even though my father was dead, the moment I obeyed the voice of God that I heard in the dream and did what God wanted me to do, I was automatically free of guilt, resentment, anger, and God's judgment.

Forgiveness can deliver you from guilt and judgment of whatever you did to someone, while unforgiveness can bind you under the bondage of guilt, anger, resentment, and God's judgment. So if you want to be free from anger, guilt, resentment, and God's judgment, then you must be willing to forgive whoever did something that hurt you.

The Bible, the Green Comb, and the Dream

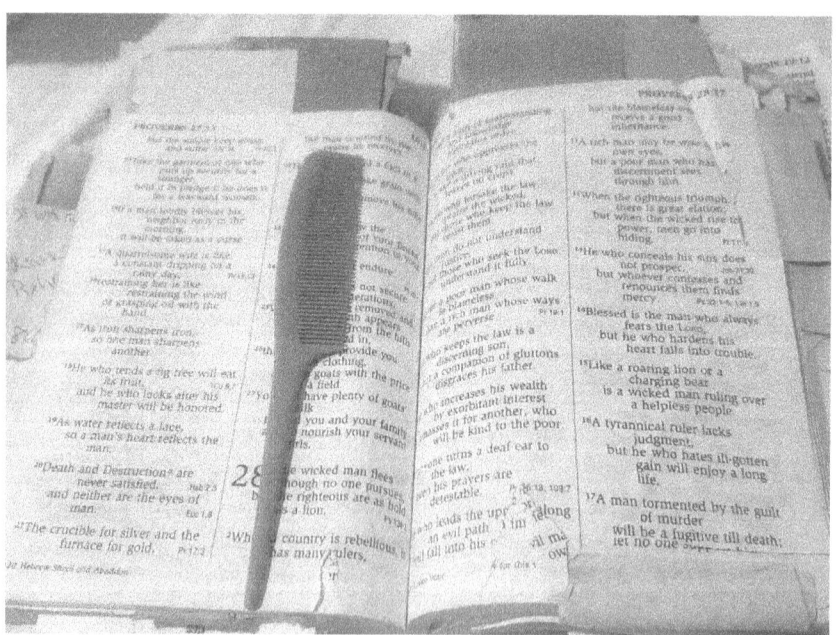

After my father's death, I went to Louisiana along with my ex-husband, my son, and a friend to help my stepmother clean my father's room. While cleaning the room, something amazing happened. My ex-husband saw a Bible, and this Bible was my late father's Bible. It was old and looked weird, but my ex-husband said, "Let me see that Bible." He took the Bible and said, "You know what? I will take this Bible home and take my time to read it from chapter to chapter and keep it for his grandson."

We returned to Texas with the Bible, laid it somewhere in the house, and forgot everything. In 2019, a woman I don't know from anywhere and who had no relationship with my father when he was alive had a dream about the Bible. This lady and I were friends on Facebook, but she did not know much about me. One day, she sent me a message and said, "I had a dream about you. Where are you? Are you alone? Can I tell you the dream now?"

I told her, "Yes, you can go ahead."

The Dream

She said, "I had a dream and saw your father in the dream. He was in an upstairs house in the room, and you were downstairs, trying to go upstairs. But there was a house downstairs that was opposite the house that your father was in. You were leaving from the house opposite the upstairs house, where there were also a group of people heading to the house that your father was in. But there was a room that was so dark, and everyone in that room was watching you as you were trying to go upstairs to your dad. And they kept saying, 'Let's see who will open that door for her to enter.' They started spying and laughing at you and watching you see who would open the door for you to go upstairs to your dad. Your dad was upstairs in the room, packing his clothes in a suitcase with his head down with tears rolling from his eyes. And I started telling him, 'It's okay, Mr. Moses. She will be fine, don't worry.' And he said to me in the dream that he left a Bible with you with a green comb in it."

ANGEL SCERE

The Meaning of the Dream

1. The upstairs' house in the dream that my father was in represents his acceptance by God in heaven into glory. God accepted him in heaven into glory because I believe strongly that he repented of his sins before his death. Your acceptance by God in heaven into glory is based on your repentance. Your repentance in forgiving someone who hurt you.

2. The dark room that was in the dream represents the darkness of unforgiveness that has been covering me over the years. Darkness represented sin, and unforgiveness was sin in the sight of God. When you find yourself in a state of unforgiveness, you are in total darkness, and when the darkness of unforgiveness is covering you, it can rob you of God's favor and blessings.

    Unforgiveness has denied many people tremendous blessings and opportunities in life. It is good to forgive because sometimes, the person to who you refuse to forgive is the one who God could use for your lifting or your recommendation for certain things that you need.

3. The people who were in the darkroom and who were laughing, spying, and watching me as I made my way to my father upstairs were wrong associates in my life, who the devil had been using to hinder me from forgiving my father, as well as making peace with him.

    There are wrong associates who the devil will always use as agents to hinder you from making peace with your loved one. You misunderstand yourself by giving contrary views and opinions about the issue that you have with your loved one or your neighbor, who you want to forgive.

    Your forgiveness toward someone who you misunderstand should not be the basis of people's opinions and views, but it must be based on personal conviction, coupled with the leading of the Holy Spirit. As a matter of fact, there are people connected to you who may not want to see you making peace with the person who you misunderstand or have a conflict with. These people are wrong associates, and therefore, you don't need views and opinions before you can forgive the person you want to forgive. Once your decision to forgive is consciously based on personal conviction, go ahead and do so, as it is the right thing to do. It should be done quickly, without seeking anyone's view or opinion.

4. The Bible in the dream that my late father left with me was an instrument of light that he wanted me to use to come out of my darkness of unforgiveness. Reading and accepting the principles of the Bible has helped me not only to forgive my late father but to also forgive other people who did things to hurt me. Whenever you find yourself in a state of unforgiveness, the best thing to do is to turn to God's book, which is the Bible, because there are principles there on forgiveness that will help you to forgive, despite the gravity of the pain that a loved one or a neighbor may have caused you.

Forgiveness, what is it all about? Why is it essential to forgive? What are the consequences of refusing to forgive? What are the benefits of forgiving?

Psychologists generally define forgiveness as a conscious, deliberate decision to release feelings of resentment or vengeance toward a person or group who has harmed you, regardless of whether they deserve your forgiveness.

There are people in this life that, when they hurt you, will not consciously realize that they have done something evil or bad to cause you pain. Humanly speaking, such people do not deserve your forgiveness. But psychologists are saying, regardless of whether the offender deserves your forgiveness, you must still forgive them for releasing yourself from anger, resentment, bitterness, and depression that might cause you a serious health problem.

Psychologically, when people reported higher levels of forgiveness, they also tended to report better health habits and decreased depression, anxiety, and anger levels. So you see, your forgiveness of someone who did something to hurt you is to your advantage of being free of health issues. Whereas your unforgiveness toward people who did things to hurt you can cause you to have serious health issues that are detrimental to your life.

What Is Forgiveness and What Is Not Forgiveness?

Forgiveness is not the force of anger, resentment, malice, and bitterness that the devil uses to destroy peace in relationships, but it is a catalyst that promotes peace and sustains peace in a relationship. Forgiveness is not the act of defending your charges or offense against the offender, but it is an act of compromising the charges to allow God to take charge of your offense.

Forgiveness is not the deception of letting go of the offense on the surface, but it is the act of letting go of the offense honestly from your heart.

Forgiveness is not about waiting on the offender to realize their offense against you before you can forgive them, but it is about forgiving them to release themselves, even if they fail to realize their offense against you.

Forgiveness is not dealing with the offender yourself, but it is about forgiving the offender and allowing God to deal with him or her. Every sustainable and lasting relationship is based on the platform of forgiveness. As a matter of fact, there will always be offenses in relationships of any kind. But what keeps a relationship moving during a crisis is forgiveness. Any relationship that lacks the attitude of forgiveness shall not survive the crisis or offense.

For instance, marriages are breaking apart, relationships are breaking apart, and institutions are crumbling globally because of the lack of forgiveness. Unforgiveness turns a small issue into a big one. It can expand and prolong a problem that is supposed to be settled early between partners in a relationship. It is better to forgive early than to delay in forgiving because the more you delay in forgiving, the more the pain and the wound of the offense can grow. And the more the pain and the wound grow, the more your life can be imprisoned by the forces of anger, resentment, and bitterness.

Why are many people finding it so difficult to forgive? Many find it difficult to forgive because they lack the characteristics that a forgiver should have toward an offender.

To be a forgiver despite painful and unbearable offenses, you must learn to cultivate the following characteristics:

1. A forgiver is one who is loving. We must develop and maintain the capacity to forgive.

   > He who is devoid of the power to forgive is devoid of the power to love. (Martin Luther King Jr.)

   Forgivers are people who strive to live like Jesus. The reason why Jesus is full of compassion and mercy is that He is loving. So to be merciful like Jesus, you must be loving like Jesus. Jesus was compassionate toward sinners. He accepted and embraced sinners. He ate with sinners because He was loving toward sinners.

   Love is a worm that can give birth to forgiveness amid offenses. Many are finding it difficult to forgive because they are finding it difficult to love. When you truly love someone, no matter the gravity of pain that person may cause you, you should still be willing to forgive him or her. This is why Dr. Martin Luther King Jr rightly said, "He who is devoid of the power to forgive is devoid of the power to love."

   If you are capable of forgiving, then you will be capable of loving; you should have the power to love. It is a contradiction to claim to love someone when you are not forgiving toward them.

2. A forgiver does not bury offenses. The act of burying offenses can prolong forgiveness in a relationship. Forgiving someone who did something to hurt you begins with the first step of expressing your grievance. True forgiveness in any relationship can take place on the platform of grievances expression. To forgive someone, you must be willing to speak out your mind and speak about your pains and hurts to free yourself.

    It took me so long to forgive my late father for the wrong things that he did to me because he was not allowing me to express my grievances. In conflict resolution, when you hinder the offender from expressing his grievances about the offense, it prolongs forgiveness.

3. A forgiver is one who is willing to compromise to let go. To forgive, you must be willing to compromise the charges and punishment of the offender to get yourself free. This is difficult to do, but it is an easier way you can forgive someone who hurt you to enjoy freedom.

    > It's not an easy journey to get to a place where you forgive people. But it is such a powerful place because it frees you. (Tyler Perry)

I am in total agreement with this quotation of the great man Tyler Perry because, for sure, it is difficult to forgive, but it is essential to forgive because there is a power in forgiveness that can set you free from the satanic forces of anger, resentment, bitterness, and so on. I never experienced freedom from guilt, anger, resentment, and bitterness until I obeyed the voice of God to forgive my late father.

If you can forgive your loved ones, your neighbor, your relatives, and whoever did something to hurt you, I can assure you that total freedom will be your portion.

CHAPTER 4

THE AGONY OF MY BROKEN MARRIAGE

My ex-husband and I lived in Côte d'Ivoire. We struggled together until the opportunity to travel to the United States of America was opened. After we had lived in the USA for a few years, he told me that he would visit his eighty-five-year-old father in Liberia without any clue that this trip was going to change my life.

Hubby left me in the United States of America and went to West Africa, specifically the Republic of Liberia, and got married to another woman. At the same time, he was still married to me. He returned from Liberia to the United States of America with a deliberate plan of divorce. To execute his plan, he intentionally started causing chaos in the home by making a mountain out of little things. He accused me falsely of living a promiscuous life and went about telling people that I was useless and not worthy of being kept as a wife. I was rejected by him and labeled as a useless woman, a fugitive, and a failure. There was no more understanding, and the marriage remained in chaos until we finally separated. Imagine your husband with whom you have lived for many years, leaving you and getting married to another woman when the two of you are still legally married.

I was abandoned by my husband after many years of marriage. The man who promised to "love, honor, and cherish me till death do us part" walked away from my life after accusing me of unimaginable things and circulating false information about me around. I felt rejected by the man I had looked up to for care and security. I was devastated and had a hard time accepting what had happened.

It is a painful and sad situation for someone to walk away from you after spending a good portion of your life with the person and doing all that you can for the marriage to work. It has a serious impact on your health. It is a stressful period that could lead to paralysis or heart attack.

Depression had me down because of his rejection. I did not understand why he did that, considering all we had been through over the years. I was broken and lonely and felt useless, unable to do anything about the situation. I could not imagine living without him by my side. Somehow, I managed to keep going because of our son, but it was a very difficult period.

It took me six years to recover from all the pains, afflictions, and frustrations that I experienced because of the treatment that I had received from my ex-husband. I was broken and depressed and had nobody to turn to during this time.

After recovering from six years of grief, pain, and afflictions, I fell into the hands of another fellow who came like an angel. Based on how he was behaving, good and nice, to me from the onset of my relationship with him, I felt that God had answered my prayers and granted my desire for a soulmate and life partner that I had been praying for. Honestly, everything was perfect from the onset. I mean, everything about my relationship with this guy, who came to replace my ex-husband, was like heaven on earth.

We had breakfast in bed, drank hot tea and chocolate at night, woke up with roses and Starbucks coffee, croissants, and eggs, as well as danced every morning and evening to love songs; chilling with wine and champagne mixed with fruits, driving around at night, taking pictures, listening to music, laughing about every little thing, and just in love. Moreover, we were obviously driving through the city's downtown beautiful bridges, viewing the sunset and skyscrapers, walking in the park, listening to music, acting crazy, and laughing. One part of the intimacy of our relationship that amazed me was soaking in the bubble bath for a few minutes while listening to music. After that, he would gently lotion my skin and braid my hair, and I thought God had sent me as an angel.

I was deeply in love with this man who came like an angel to replace my ex-husband to the point where I acted stupidly in some ways in relation to him. Sometimes, when you allow your love for someone to control you in a relationship, it can make you do some stupid things and think you are doing the right thing amid your stupidity.

On several occasions, this man lied to me and deceived me; but the lie and deception that really broke my heart and made me lose confidence in him were when he told me that he and his sister were going on a business trip. I later discovered that he was in Liberia, intending to engage a girl who had just given birth to a child for him. After these lies, deceptions, and games, should I keep trusting him and loving him? The answer is an absolute no! I can't keep trusting him and loving him because if I do so, it will be to my own detriment.

CHAPTER 5

THE TRAUMA OF ABANDONMENT

I was abandoned not once but thrice by people who were very dear to me. First, my mother, who just placed me in a box and left me at the door of my dad's apartment like she was delivering goods, even though he was not at home. She did not care whether or not something happened to me, or she would not have left me there when my dad was not around. She just dumped me and went her way. Her actions suggest that she did not love me. Unbelievable for a mother.

Growing up without my mother around, I did not believe then that her departure was permanent, but I can safely conclude that it is with the passage of time. She has not come around since that fateful day to provide any explanation, and I have been left with so many unanswered questions. How can a woman who carried a child in her womb for nine months abandon the child? Did I do something wrong? What good reason could a parent leave his or her child and not look back?

Deeply wounded by her actions, I have struggled with shame and guilt over the years. I have painfully wondered if something is wrong with me; and if I am unworthy of love. I have not been able to absorb the enormity of her action. As a mother, she should be there to love and care for her child or children the most, but instead, she consciously and voluntarily walked away from her responsibilities.

The effect of rejection is devastating. The fact that my mother didn't want me, has caused me so much pain. It has been very difficult for me to accept. She has remained a somber figure that haunts my life like a nightmare.

My dad sent me to his mother, who was unable to provide for me. He went about having fun with several women and finally settled down with one woman who had two children for him. Besides those two, there were twelve of us. However, he neglected the rest of us and only supported the children of his wife. Whenever I attempted to raise the issue with him, he flared up. As a result of his refusal to hear me out and do something about the situation, our relationship became strained, and we did not speak to each other for a long time.

Once again, I felt rejected and became very angry with my dad. I did not forgive him up to his death. It is not easy to accept that your father, your ideal role model alongside your mother, doesn't stay in your life. Parents are supposed to value and enjoy their children. If the one who is meant to love and care for you the most in this world leaves you, it becomes very difficult to believe that anyone and everyone who becomes important to you will not do the same.

Then the man who promised to "love, honor, and cherish me till death do us part" selfishly walked out on our son and me for another woman. I was so bitter and just wanted to be left alone, but I had to keep going because of my son. I barely ate any food for a good while. I was miserable and could only wonder why it was happening to me. Was it wrong for me to have committed all my time to being a wife to him, preparing meals, doing his laundry, keeping the home, and taking care of him and our son?

The sheep in wolf clothing who came into my life after my ex-husband's departure, like an angel, also went walking. Did he pretend to be in love with me because he needed me at the time?

After these incidents, I wondered if I was cursed. Why does the same thing keep happening to me? Am I not good enough to be loved and cherished? Am I only good enough to fulfill their needs?

CHAPTER 6

VICTIM OF STIGMATIZATION

I struggled with trust, shame, and low self-esteem for a long time. The conspicuous absence of my parents tormented my life. Whenever someone asked about my parents, I would respond vaguely because it was embarrassing. How do you explain that your parents did not care about you? When your parents are not giving you the love, care, and support they ought to, people do not value you. They tend to treat you like trash.

Some people around me did not make the situation any easier. They made remarks that only elevated my pain. Some looked into my face and said I would be useless all the days of my life. Some said nothing good would come from out of me. Some said I would be a failure in life and so on. But I am glad that man's destiny is in the hands of the Almighty God and not man. His word states, "For I know the thoughts that I think toward you, says the Lord, thoughts of peace and not of evil, to give you a future and a hope" (Jeremiah 29:11 NKJV).

The exit of my husband only caused people to scrutinize me more. It was like the icing on top of the cake. People began to judge me just by what they heard. They looked at me with disdain and made all kinds of derogatory remarks. I lost many opportunities and found it hard to make friends or keep relationships. Men would suddenly change their minds after proposing to me. This made me so ashamed that I felt like a failure. The breakup was damaging to me.

CHAPTER 7

GOD'S MIRACLES ARE REAL

Don't give up before the miracle happen.
—Fannie Flagg

At what point in your life do you need a miracle? When your doctor says you have cancer and within seven days you will die? Do you need a miracle from God? Will you remain indoors fasting, praying and seeking God's intervention for fourteen days when you have seven days to live? What do you do when all the people you relied on for survival turn their backs on you?

Are you going to believe God for a miracle, or are you going to commit suicide? What do you do when your husband hangs up his phone on you after ten years of marriage and leaves you and your children to go and live with another woman with whom he is in love? Are you going to believe God for a miracle or give up? What do you do when the economy of your country is faced with crises beyond your human control? Are you going to blame the government, or are you going to believe God for a miracle?

Your answers to these questions, in a positive sense, validate the fact of whether you believe in the reality of God's miracles. Miracles are real. Miracles do happen. Our God, Yahweh, is a miracle-working God.

If miracles are real, then what is a miracle? A miracle, according to the many definitions, is an amazing or unusual event that no man or law can explain. It always leaves people wondering as to why and how it happened when the prevailing circumstances suggest that it should be another way. It is beyond human understanding and shows the divine intervention of supernatural power.

A miracle is not what man does, but it is the doing of God. A miracle is something that scientists cannot understand, as brilliant as they are, because it is based on the exercising of your faith in God.

The exercising of your faith in God is what guarantees the release of God's miracles in your life. Remember, the scripture says, "All things are possible to them that believe" (Mark 9:23).

Faith is the platform on which divine possibilities take place in your life. It takes your faith in God to prove your doctor's report wrong concerning your health. It takes your faith in God to keep praying for a miracle, for a solution, and for a way out of a crisis. The miracle-working God does not easily perform miracles unless you believe without a doubt that He is able to do that which you are asking of Him. He always works miracles within the confines of faith. Therefore, you must believe whenever you need a miracle from God. There are lots of horrible experiences that I have had throughout my life's journey. From the very beginning of my existence, when I was just a baby, up to my adult life. I have survived all the horrible experiences in my life through the miracles of God.

I was only a few months old when I was placed in a cartoon by my mother and left at the door of my late father's apartment, based on some misunderstanding between her and my dad. My dad was at work when my mother arrived there with me, but she still left me in the cartoon at the door of his apartment. A neighbor passing by saw the cartoon at the door with a baby crying in it. She contacted my dad, who was at work, to inform him about what she had seen. Shocked by the information he had received, he left work early to see for himself what the neighbor was talking about. Upon his arrival, he met me lying in a cartoon at the entrance to his apartment. He was at the time not in the position to take care of me as he was a single man and had to work. He, therefore, quickly called his mom and asked her to please take me to her house to live with her and take care of me.

Something could have happened to me between the time that my mother dropped me off and when my dad's neighbor saw me. It was the special grace of God that preserved me. That same grace that saved me is still available for you today.

God saved me because He has a plan and purpose for my life, which is unfolding gradually. My mom apparently did not have a personal relationship with God, and neither did not understand that. Somehow, God directed my dad, and he had his mom take me to live with her.

Abandonment is painful, but it is not the end of the world. A man may reject or abandon you, but it does not mean that it is the end for you. Our heavenly father is the only one with the final saying. That's why He is called the Alpha and Omega. His plans for your destiny will ripen at the set time.

There are times when God permits you to experience some things for various reasons. It could be to show His power and might, to show us the people around us, or to draw us closer to Him. Whatever the reason, we do not always understand it while we are going through stuff, but gradually we do and begin to appreciate what we have been through.

Today I am engaged in activities that are impacting lives positively. So many people are looking up to me. So do not bother when you are rejected by people. They are mere humans and not God! Your destiny is beyond them. Besides that, even Jesus Christ, the greatest man who lived on earth, was rejected by the very people whom He came from heaven to save. He had a purpose for coming to earth, and it had to be fulfilled and was fulfilled. No man can stop God's purpose for your life.

Therefore, do not be deterred by man's actions or attitude toward you. Know that you are a child of God, and he has a plan and purpose for your being on earth.

Acknowledge and trust Him in all that you do and He will direct your path and bless you in the presence of your enemies.

My mom should have been the last person on earth to have abandoned me. Perhaps, if she knew that God had great plans for me, she may have managed with me. Yes, she abandoned me, but God did not. He was there for me and still is, as promised in Psalm 27:10, that when my father and mother forsake me, He will take me. Many years later, God showed up for me again when I was in a difficult situation. I was pregnant and had developed complications. The situation was serious to the extent that my baby and I were not expected to live. A decision had to be made about which one of us would live. Keeping His promise in Deuteronomy 31:6, not to leave us nor forsake us, God intervened and saved both of our lives. This was indeed a miracle because had it not been for the divine intervention of God, I may not have been alive today. He is indeed a miracle-working God and a promise keeper.

It was during the summer season when one of my friends came to my home for a visit. She suggested that we go and visit a friend in downtown Dallas. While we were on our way, the car we were riding broke down in the middle of the road. We quickly got a tow truck to get her car to the shop.

We also got into the tow truck, but because of the bouncing of the tow truck, my baby started moving around in my belly and going up to my chest. My water broke, and I was rushed to the hospital. At that time, my pregnancy was about five months. The doctor had to put artificial water in me and ordered bed rest for me. They had me on medication to buy time for the child to at least reach any stage that would've been safe for survival.

While I was on bed rest, I was running a temperature, so it wasn't safe for the child. The doctor decided to give me an epidural to force the labor so the child would not get sick because they did not want to risk anything. I was due May 18, but I had the baby on February 27, about three months earlier. The baby was only one pound, as nothing was really developed because of his early arrival.

My child was born amid a throng of nurses and doctors because of how terrible his condition was. The truth is that my son, Ted, was at the point of death. Physically, I didn't see the doctors and the nurses working on him, but consciously, we knew that it was God who miraculously delivered him. While Ted was in the ICU, we had his baby shower because he came earlier than his due date.

Ted was to be born on May 18, 2006. But instead, he was born on February 27, 2006. But that date was special to me because I arrived in America from Africa on February 27, 2005. So to me, it was miraculous. God knew exactly what he was doing. God can never make mistakes.

Ted stayed in the hospital for six months because he was not breathing on his own. His body was underdeveloped, and neither were his lungs. But what is interesting here is that within the six months, God's watchful eyes were opened to my son day and night. I strongly believe that angels were on assignment twenty-four hours of the day, seeing to it that nothing went wrong with my son's life. And it's no wonder why he came out safe from the hospital and is still alive today. The expectation of the enemies was to see my child dead, but God proved them wrong.

When you trust God to handle things for you, the enemies will stumble and not prevail against you. They will be greatly ashamed, for the Lord God of Israel, who never loses a battle, will be with you. The scripture says, "If God is for you, who shall be against you" (Romans 8:31).

After God intervened and saved our lives, another round of anxiety started. My son's breathing was not stable. Every time he was scheduled to go home, he would stop breathing and had to be attended to and kept for a few more days for observation. This went on for a while before the doctors determined that he needed to undergo surgery because of his instability in breathing before he could be released. He was quickly taken to the Cook Children's Medical Center for the surgery. This is when I almost lost faith and hope in God. I started asking Him how an infant on breathing tubes fighting for his life could undergo surgery? I thought God was punishing me because it didn't make any sense to me. I was giving up. As God would have it, the doctors did the surgery, and it was successful to the glory of God.

Many days when I think about things that I have been through and going through, it makes me think that God is punishing me for something my parents did or one of my ancestors did, and I had to be the one to face the consequences for them. But now, I have realized that He was preparing me for something bigger than myself. I began to understand after I started talking to people and encouraging them to stand firm and keep pressing on, as life is indeed worth living.

I believe the devil and his agents fought my son so badly during his conception in my womb and his birth because they saw greatness in him. Know that Satan and his agents cannot fight anyone who is not carrying a seed of greatness inside of them. So the enemies are tirelessly fighting you because you are impregnated with the seed of greatness. The good news is that no matter how your enemies fight you, that seed of greatness that God deposited in you can never die. You must give birth to it. The enemies have been doing all they can get in every possible way to abort your destiny, but your destiny cannot be aborted because it is a matter of must that you give birth to destiny.

CHAPTER 8

I PUT MY PAST BEHIND ME

*Change is the law of life. And those who look only
to the past or present are certain to miss the future.*
—John F. Kennedy

The past has to do with a time before the present. The past is something that is no longer exists or happening. In a positive sense, your past could be used as a testimony to build your courage and your confidence in facing the challenges of the present. Whereas in a negative sense, the devil and his agents can use your past in the present to kill your future.

My emphasis in this chapter is not on your past being used in a positive sense of building up your courage and your confidence to face challenges in the present that may hinder you from actualizing your future, but on the unscrupulous habit of the devil using your past to kill your future. The great man, John F. Kennedy, said, "Looking only to the past or the present can make you miss the glorious future that God has for you."

I absolutely agree with him because when you keep thinking about your horrible experiences of the past, it can deny you access to all the good things that the future has to offer you.

When you allow the devil and his agents to keep reminding you about the bad experiences of the past, it will arouse in you the feeling of guilt, regret, frustration, and hopelessness. And when you start developing these negative feelings, depression sets in, and you are distracted from accomplishing your goals.

Satan reminds you of your past to build in you a negative mindset of something bad that happened to you in the past. The fact that you lost your relationship in the past does not, in any way, mean that you cannot have a new relationship again. The fact that you lost your job in the past does not mean that you can never get a new job now or in the future.

God has been and is always in the business of doing something new in your life. But the truth is that you can never experience a new beginning in your life until you forget the former things of disappointment in a relationship, the loss of your marriage, being abandoned by your parents or guardians, a sponsor, or a friend who you had been looking up to for everything to survive, and so on.

Until you can forget the former things, you can never experience the move of God in the present. And until you experience the move of God in your life in the present, you can never actualize your desired future. The future is not for those who are focusing on the former things of the past but for those who are focusing on constructing their lives in the present, despite the challenges of the past, in order to position themselves for what the future holds.

As a matter of fact, when you stay in the frustrated and regrettable state of destructive experiences of the past, you are denied access to what the future may hold for you. Moreover, the devil can remind you of the horrible experiences of your past, not only to develop in you the feelings of negativism but to also create an atmosphere of sadness around you. And once you find yourself in a state of sadness, it can obviously hinder you from experiencing the miracles. The manifestation of God's miracles in your life is based on the maintenance of the atmosphere of joy, praise, and thanksgiving.

Paul and Silas experienced the miracles of being delivered from prison by an earthquake because they maintained an atmosphere of praise and thanksgiving (Acts 16:25). Many people desire a miracle from Him, but they are never thankful or joyful, and neither are they full of the praises of God. They are finding it difficult to develop the heart of thanksgiving because they have given room to the devil to remind them of bad experiences of their past.

I have had a lot of horrible experiences in the past that I've been sharing with you in previous chapters of this book, but I have chosen to put my past behind me. And therefore, I am breaking forth day after day in the present. If you want to experience a breaking forth in the present, then you must be willing to put your past behind you. I put the past behind me in the following ways:

1. I put the past behind me by overcoming guilt. Living with a guilty conscience about something you did wrong, intentionally or accidentally, in the past can hinder you from moving on with your life in the present.

What is guilt? Guilt is a feeling people typically have after doing something wrong, intentionally or accidentally. Living with a guilty conscience about something wrong that you did to someone in the past or present can create an atmosphere of worry, depression, doubt, and shame. Take note of the keywords here. *Worry, depression, doubt, and shame.* Worry is the product of living with a guilty conscience about something wrong that you did to someone in the past or the present. And when you start to worry because of something wrong that you did to a friend, a neighbor, or a loved one, your worry can consequently cause a depression that will envelop your life. When the peace of the Lord is lacking, it hinders your mind from functioning to a maximum productive level in working toward achieving your goals, as well as actualizing your goals and your dreams.

Know that the functioning of your mind to a maximum productive level is based on the maintenance of the peace of God in your life. This is because the scriptures say, "The peace of the Lord is what surpasses all understanding" (Philippians 4:7). It enables your mind to function accurately in understanding and dealing with issues that you may be confronted with.

Satan is always roaming, looking for ways to enter our lives. It is, therefore, necessary to read the word of God daily so that we can draw near to the Almighty, who alone is able to keep us from falling. By reading the word, we also become familiar with God's promises, and our faith is strengthened. When Satan attempts to tamper with us, we can confidently order him to get behind us and take his hands out of our affairs. If our faith is weak, when we are going through difficulties, we will not know what to do, and Satan will then manipulate our minds. We will begin to feel guilty and worry instead of praying. This is detrimental to one's health as depression will set in, leading to all kinds of other stuff.

Living with a guilty conscience hinders your ability to tap into the blessings that God has in store for you. It also paralyzes your faith. You are constantly doubting your ability to do things instead of moving forward. If you believe that you wronged someone, go and find the person, apologize and ask for their forgiveness. If he or she refuses to accept your apology, take it to the Lord in prayer. Based on my experience with my dad, I am of the conviction that the Lord will forgive you if you sincerely ask Him to, even if the person you supposedly offended did not. You should then forgive yourself and move on with your life.

At this point, you would have done the best that you could. If you do not forgive yourself, you will not have peace of mind as you won't be able to concentrate on the things that you are doing. When you can't concentrate, you may not get desired results, and this may frustrate you all the more. You will continue tormenting yourself by living in the past. It is, therefore, important to forgive yourself so that you can be relieved of the stress and other associated problems.

2. I put my past behind me by removing my eyes and mind from closed doors.

Keeping your eyes on doors that have been closed can prevent you from benefiting from current open doors. Know that God opens some doors before you on a seasonal basis, and when your season of benefiting from them is over, He closes them to open new ones. You lost the job because God did not intend for it to be a permanent one for you but rather a seasonal job. When the time that He wanted you to spend on that job was over, He took it away from you. Perhaps, He took it away to bless you with a better job that will give you more financial benefits. He knows what is best.

The man or the woman walked out of the relationship or the marriage probably, because the two of you were not meant to stay together as life partners. God permitted me to experience it, and I believe that it was for a good cause. It hurt me that my husband walked away after everything that we had been through. However, his leaving caused me to know God as I had never known Him before.

I was in terrible shape after he left. Nothing around me seemed to be working, and I did not understand why. But God was in control as always. His plan for my life did not align with what was happening around me. That is the constant confusion that had become the new code of conduct of my ex-husband. He looked for every little opportunity to stir up something. It was becoming unbearable.

As God is not a God of confusion, He intervened, and the man walked out of the marriage. My spiritual life may not have developed up to the level where it is now had we remained together because of all the confusion. During those dark hours, I spent a lot of time in the presence of God, and it helped me. This is something I rarely did prior to this problem with my ex-husband. I learned that only God is faithful to keep promises and to look up to Him alone.

God is able to take you through. So do not fear when someone walks away from you or ridicules you. Turn the matter over to Jesus and move on with your life. Do not continue to delay your progress by reliving memories of yesterday. It will only cause you to hurt more. What the person may have done to you tells a lot about their character and does not define you. Trust God without a doubt, and He will definitely see you through.

Guilt Causes Shame

Shame is a painful mental feeling aroused by having done something dishonorable or ridiculous. Shame is derived from a loss of respect, value, and integrity because of some ridiculous things that you may have done. Shame is dangerous because it cuts you off from your relatives and loved ones and drives you away from your environment into another environment.

Shame keeps you in the cave of regret and absolution, and when care is not taken, it might even lead you to commit suicide. Gossip and accusations are the two forces that can increase feelings of shame. The more people gossip about you and accuse you of something that you have done or that you never did, the more you develop feelings of shame. I have been accused falsely by people about things that I never did, and the false accusations and gossip by my critics created an atmosphere of shame in my life. A shame that could have driven me away from my African community, but I overcame every form of shame by overcoming the feelings of guilt. Shame is caused by guilt, and so to overcome shame, you must fight to overcome the feelings of guilt.

Guilt Can Diminish Self-Esteem

Your self-esteem has to do with you developing a sense of worth and value in yourself. The truth is that the level to which you build your self-esteem is the level to which people hold you in high esteem. On the contrary, when you hold yourself in low esteem, people will also hold you in low esteem. To hold yourself in high esteem, you must be willing to do all that you can to protect and respect yourself.

It is often said that if you have respect for yourself, people will, in return, show you respect. Another way that you can build your self-esteem is by overcoming guilt. There is nothing that can diminish your self-esteem compared to guilt.

Our enemy, the devil, is always in the unscrupulous habit of using your guilty conscience for something wrong that you did in the past intentionally or accidentally to diminish your self-esteem. In Revelation 12:10, Satan is described as the accuser of the brethren. The devil will always accuse you of something wrong that you did in the past or in the present to make you feel guilty. And when you acquiesce to his accusation and develop feelings of guilt, he consequently uses your guilty conscience to decrease your self-esteem.

Pastor Chris Oyakhilome, in one of his articles in his book, *Rhapsody of Realities,* said, "Sin consciousness is the devil's strategy to make you feel unworthy before God."

To be sin-conscious means to feel guilty about your sin, even when you have been forgiven by God, your creator. When you are guilty of sin, it makes you feel unworthy before God and your fellow men, and when you develop a feeling of unworthiness, it diminishes or decreases your self-esteem.

Overcoming Guilt

I am a victim of guilt. I suffered severely from guilt in the past for years, but I overcame it by applying the following principles, the principle of refusing to accept the accusation of the devil and his agents. Satan and his agents are faithful to their assignments of accusing you of things that you did in the past or the present, knowingly or unknowingly, to make you feel guilty before God and your fellow men. So if you want to overcome guilt, then you must refuse to accept the accusations of the devil.

Whenever the devil tries to accuse you of something sinful that you did in the past or the present, remind him that the blood of Jesus on the cross has cleansed you from your sin. Whenever the devil tries to accuse you of sin to make you feel guilty, remind him that on the cross, the Lord Jesus said, "It is finished!" Remind the devil that the scripture says, "If you confess your sin, God is faithful and just to forgive you and cleanse you from all unrighteousness" (1 John 1:9 KJV).

If you want to overcome guilt, you must be willing to refuse to accept the accusation of the devil. You can overcome guilt by being self-forgiving. You must learn to forgive yourself, even if somebody whom you offended refuses to forgive you. There are people in this life who will never forgive you for something you did to hurt them.

You can't afford to feel guilty because of their unforgiveness toward you, but what you can do is ask God to forgive you and also forgive yourself and move on with your life. This is how you can overcome guilt to live a life of freedom and fulfillment.

Seven Ways of Overcoming Your Past

1. Don't allow the memories of your past to be used against the realities of your future.

   > I use memories, but I will not allow memories to use me. (Deepak Chopra)

2. Be grateful and thankful for the things that happened to you in the past.

   > I am looking forward to the future and feeling grateful for the past. (Mike Rowe)

3. Don't burden yourself with the past. Instead, free yourself of the past to move on with your life in the present.

   > The past is a stepping stone, not a millstone. (Robber Plant)

4. Never allow your past experiences to dictate the present realities of your life that guarantee the actualization of your future.

   > The past has no power over the present moment. (Eckhart Tolle)

5. Be ready always to resist the negative ideas and feelings of the past.

   > When we are tired, we are attacked by ideas we conquered long ago. (Friedrich Nietzsche)

6. Forget about the painful experiences of the past and focus on the dreams of the future.

>I like the dreams of the future better than the history of the past. (Thomas Jefferson)

7. Never contemplate or meditate on horrible experiences of the past.

>What's done is done. (Hilliard Macbeth)

CHAPTER 9

I DID OVERCOME AND CAME OUT OF MY VALLEY OF UNBEARABLE EXPERIENCES

My life journey has been rocky over the years. I have had a lot of horrible experiences that could have taken my life away. I discussed some of these horrible experiences in previous chapters; nevertheless, I would like to highlight them in this chapter. I would like to begin the list with my abandonment as a baby of tender age by my mom in a cartoon. At this point in my life, my grandmother came in and rescued me by taking me to the village to live with her. I grew up as a child, struggling with my grandmother in a village that is geographically located in Bawin, Maryland County, Republic of Liberia, West Africa.

After a couple of years of my village life experience, my grandmother and I were driven away from Liberia into exile (Ivory Coast) by the Liberian civil war. While my grandmother and I were on the Ivory Coast, we also had challenges that were beyond our human control.

Grandmother got seriously sick and lost her life consequently as a result of the sickness. I was left alone in the Ivory Coast as an orphan, struggling for a better life, but during my struggles, the Lord made a way for me, and today, I am residing in the USA (United States of America).

Apart from the horrible experiences that I had as a child growing up, I have also had some heartbreaking experiences as a young girl with my marriage and with some forces who wanted to see me down in life.

I got married at a very youthful stage of my life, and unfortunately, after a couple of years, I lost my marriage because of some marital crisis that was beyond my human control.

Since the loss of my marriage, I have experienced several relationship crises that resulted in me being mocked and becoming the talk of the town. If gossip could kill then and now, I would have been dead and gone.

Like Hannah in the Bible, who experienced the agony of gossip and mockery by her mate, Peninnah, and her neighbor because of her barrenness and refused to give attention to all the horrible things that people were saying about her, but rather prayerfully called upon the Almighty God; I, too, learned to never mind the things that people say or think about me, as it relates to the several relationship crises of my life and other issues that I had been faced with during the course of my life's journey.

The truth is that, once you are still alive, people will talk about you. Some will talk about good things about you, and some will talk about bad things about you based on their opinion about you. You can't stop them from talking because this is something that you don't have control over. So just allow them to keep talking.

On the other hand, don't mind what people are saying about you, but instead, concern yourself with who the word of God says you are. As a matter of fact, your critics don't have the final say concerning your life. Only God in heaven has the final say. Your critics can say all the worst things about you but never mind them because the Lord God Almighty is the alpha and omega.

They can call you all the worst names: good for nothing, prostitute, smoker, drunkard, drug addict, etc., but never mind them because only God has the final say.

I remember the dark days of my struggles as a village girl in Liberia and later being an orphan on the Ivory Coast. My critics thought the worst about me and said the worst things about me. Some literally looked into my face and told me that I would be useless all the days of my life. Some said nothing good would come from out of me. Some said I would be a failure in life and so on. But I am truly grateful to God for proving them wrong. Whenever you are reading this book, I prophetically declare over your life that God will prove your enemies wrong and put them to shame in the name of Jesus.

I Overcame at Last! Who Are Overcomers?

Overcomers are people who succeed in dealing with the issues of life that confront them as a result of the consistent attack of their enemies. Overcomers deal with the problems and the issues that they are confronted with by means of spiritual warfare and not physical warfare. Remember, the scripture says, "We wrestle not against flesh and blood, but against principalities, against powers, against the rulers of the darkness of this world, against spiritual wickedness in high places" (Ephesians 6:12 KJV).

Overcomers overcome the issues that are confronting their lives by spiritual warfare and not by physical warfare. This is because the principalities and the power that are afflicting your life with sicknesses, diseases, hardship, disappointment, and failure are not physically afflicting you but spiritually. Most of the troubles and catastrophes that you experience in your personal life, in your family, with your job, and in your career are a result of the attack of demons who are assigned to your life. Know that demons are spirits, and therefore, they attack people spiritually and not physically. So to overcome them, you must position yourself spiritually and also attack them spiritually.

Your spiritual warfare against the forces of darkness is in three dimensions—the prayer dimension, the fasting dimension, and the praise dimension. When you engage yourself in spiritual warfare by these three dimensions, demons assigned to your personal life, as well as to your family, will have no option but to pack and leave.

Despite all the heartbreaking challenges and experiences that I have had in my life, I overcame them at last through spiritual warfare. I overcame at last because, in the midst of my challenges, I developed the attitude of an overcomer. There are basically seven attitudes of an overcomer that you must develop if you want to overcome the challenges that you are faced with right now in your life. They are as follows:

1. An overcomer is one who is proactive and not reactive.

   If you are proactive, you make things happen instead of waiting for them to happen to you. Active means "doing something." The prefix *pro* means before. So if you are proactive, you are ready before something happens.

   Stop waiting on people to make things happen for you, and take a step of faith to make things happen for yourself. The miracle that you are expecting from God will take place by awakening your spirit to move toward doing something meaningful and productive with yourself. You can never experience the manifestation of your expectations by sitting but by getting up and moving.

   For instance, a healing evangelist can say to a cripple man in a wheelchair, "I command you to walk in the name of Jesus Christ!" However, it is by that cripple man taking a step of faith to rise that will make him experience the miracle of walking and jumping like he never did before.

   Overcomers are proactive and not reactive. The opposite of being proactive is to be reactive. To be reactive means to wait for things to unfold before responding. To be an overcomer amid your crisis, the secret is to stop waiting on things to happen for you but instead move by faith to make them happen.

2. An overcomer is someone who will never give up in life.

> Overcomers are people with a strong faith who can refuse to give up in the midst of crisis based on the faith in God. (Erasmus G. Jarkloh)

One of the secrets that can make you overcome challenges and difficulties is to refuse to give up. Overcomers are not quitters, and quitters are not overcomers.

> Overcomers are people who can refuse to give up amid crisis based on their faith in God. (Erasmus G. Jackson)

Overcomers are people who cultivate a forceful attitude, coupled with perseverance and endurance in facing the issues confronting them. Do not be deterred by difficulties because they are part of life. The Bible tells us that challenges will come, but if we trust God, He will be with us and see us through.

There are basically two major characteristics of overcomers that make them stand firm and not waiver amid crisis.

a. They are full of courage and confidence. Overcomers are always full of courage and confidence that God can pull them out of their struggles and difficulties.

b. Overcomers are people with faith. They always believe that God can deliver them from their afflictions and give them victory over their enemies. If you want to be an overcomer who will refuse to give up in the midst of your affliction, then you must possess these two characteristics.

3. Overcomers are not negative in their thinking about their circumstances.

　　Overcomers are always positive in their thinking and not negative. They don't think negatively of being victims of their circumstances, but they think positively of being victorious over their circumstances. The outcome of your circumstance in life is based on your thinking. If you think negatively about your circumstances, you could get a negative outcome. Whereas when you think positively about your circumstances, you could get a positive outcome.

　　Be careful about the thought patterns that you develop in your life because everything that goes on in your mind begins with your thoughts. Your success begins with your thoughts, whereas failure of any kind in your life can also begin with your thoughts. Solomon, the wise man, said, "As a man thinketh in his heart so is he" (Proverbs 23:7).

　　As a man thinketh so is he, simply means that you cannot excel above your thoughts. You can only live your life according to the limit of your thinking. To live a better life, you must think highly of yourself. Neither can you think highly of yourself and live the life of a pauper.

　　The problem with many people around the globe is that they devalue themselves. Many people are living a very low standard of life that God never intended them to live because of how they perceive themselves. Some people have developed the mindset of living in a one-bedroom apartment all the days of their life when God's plan for them is to live in a mansion.

　　Some people have developed the wrong mindset of being single all their life because of their disappointments in past relationships when God's plan for their life is to get married and live happily with their spouses. God is not thinking low of you, so don't think low of yourself. You must learn to bring your thoughts in alignment with God's thoughts for your life. Overcomers are people who think the way God is thinking. So if you must be an overcomer, then you're thinking must be in line with God's thinking for your life. I overcame amid all the horrible experiences that I have been sharing with you in this book because I was positive in my thinking about my circumstances and not negative.

4. An overcomer is one who has the attitude of a warrior and not a coward.

    Life is a journey of battles, and the battles of life will never end until you leave this world. Once you are still alive as a child of God, you must expect to battle with people in your family and outside of your family. You must expect to face a battle with people at your job site and elsewhere, the battle of choosing major decisions in life at the crossroad of decision-making and so on. Life is a journey that consists of different kinds of battles, and if you want to overcome the battles of your life journey, then you must be a warrior and not a coward.

    David in the Bible overcame, amid all his battles, with his enemies because he was a warrior and not a coward. Remember, he started being a warrior in his youth. As a young boy taking care of his father's sheep, one day, a lion came to attack the sheep. And as a warrior, David stood firm with courage and killed the lion. On another day, a bear came to attack the sheep, and David fought the bear and killed it.

    David never ran from the lion, nor did he run from the bear, but he stood firm and killed them because he was a warrior. Warriors don't run from their enemies, but they stand firm with confidence and courage to fight them. Stop running from the enemies in your family, at your job site, and in your community but stand firm to fight them. You can stand firm to fight back because, in Christ Jesus, you are a warrior and not a coward.

Your fight against your enemies is not in your human strength, but it's in the strength of Jesus. On another occasion, David's father sent him with food for his brothers to the camp of the army of Israel, and upon the arrival of David, he saw Goliath challenging the army of Israel. He quickly ran to someone and asked, "What will be given to the person who will kill this so-called giant who is defying the army of the living God?" (1 Samuel 17:26 NKJV)

He was given the price and the benefits of killing Goliath. With no delay, he embarked upon a fight of killing Goliath, and finally with the help of God, he brought down Goliath. You see, David overcame the lion and the bear that came to attack his father's sheep. He also fought and overcame Goliath by killing him because he was a warrior and not a coward. To be an overcomer amid the battles of life, you must be a warrior and not a coward.

5. An overcomer is positive in his confession in the midst of crisis.

> Overcomers don't speak the language of pessimism, but they speak the language of optimism. (Erasmus G. Jarkloh)

To be an overcomer amid the crisis of life, you must be positive in your confession and not negative. Negative happening is always the outcome of a negative confession, whereas positive happening in your life is the outcome of a positive confession. Negative confession kills your courage and your confidence, thereby hindering you from overcoming the crisis of life, whereas positive confession builds up your courage and your confidence and enables you to overcome the issues of your life.

God has given you the tongue that you have in your mouth to use it to your advantage and not to your disadvantage. You can use your tongue to your advantage when you are using it to speak positive things about your life, whereas you can use it to your disadvantage when you are speaking negative things about your life.

Overcomers are not negative in their confession, and therefore, if you want to overcome challenging situations, you must be positive in your confession. Never allow your challenges to change your confession. There are lots of unbearable challenges that I've been experiencing in my life journey, but notwithstanding my challenges, I've always been positive in my confession. And therefore, I am overcoming it day after day.

In the environment of overcoming, you don't hear people saying, "I don't think I will make it." But you hear them saying, with boldness, "That no matter what comes my way, I will make it in Jesus's name." You don't hear people saying, "The doctor said she has fourteen days to live." But you hear people saying with confidence, "God will prove the doctor's report wrong. She will survive the sickness and keep living on." This is how people talk in the environment of overcomers. My prayer for you is that you will stay in the environment of overcomers. People who speak positively based on their courage and their confidence in God refuse to stay in the environment of pessimism. Cowards are people who speak negatively about their circumstances out of fear and lack of faith in God to pull them out.

6. An overcomer is one who is spiritually aware of who he is in Christ Jesus and not ignorant of himself.

Many are finding it so difficult to overcome challenges they are confronted with in life because they are ignorant of who they are in Christ Jesus. When you are ignorant of whom you are, Satan and his agents can take advantage of messing with you and everything attached to you.

You are not ordinary, but you are extraordinary. You are not a victim but a victor. You were not born into this world to be a victim of circumstances, but you were born to be victorious over circumstances. Therefore, you must live with the consciousness that you are a victor and not a victim.

As a child of God, the scripture describes us as a chosen people, a royal priesthood, a holy nation, and God's special possession, that you may declare the praises of him who called you out of darkness into his wonderful light.

You are a royal priesthood because, by your salvation and experience, you have been born into a royal family, which is the family of Christ Jesus. You can't be meat for the devil, and neither can you be a victim of sicknesses, frustration, disappointments, setbacks, and failures because you are part of a royal family. Jesus Christ, the king of this family, oversees the affairs of your life.

Others will complain and cry about the economic crisis of your nation. They will complain of scarcity; some will even die of diseases and sicknesses. But as for you, you can never be a victim of such things because the King of kings oversees the affairs of life. Not only is He in charge of the affairs of your life, but He lives in you. And His presence is with you twenty-four hours of the day, seven days of the week, four weeks of the month, and three hundred and sixty-five days of the year.

The fact that the glorious presence of the Lord Jesus is with you, and the fear of being defeated by your enemies should have no place in your life, but rather you should always be cognizant of the fact that you are an overcomer in every situation. Therefore, you must talk like an overcomer and walk like an overcomer.

One of the secrets of you overcoming whatever you are dealing with is to rely on the promises of God Almighty without doubting and to be knowledgeable of who you are in Christ. During my dark days of pain and afflictions, I did not give up; instead, I overcame because I was cognizant of who I was. Even though I was experiencing severe suffering, despite my despair, I knew who I was. I knew that I was a woman with purpose and destiny, and therefore, I never allowed the devil to use my sufferings to influence me into compromising my godly standard of living.

If you are an overcomer who knows who you are and what your purpose of living is, then, of course, no matter how difficult things may get in your life, you would never compromise your worth, values, and God's biblical standard of living for your life.

7. An overcomer is one who believes that God can do it even when it seems impossible.

To be an overcomer when surrounded by problems, you must cultivate the attitude of believing and not doubting. Doubt is not an issue for overcomers, whereas faith is an instrument that builds up their courage and their confidence and enables them to overcome. Without faith in God, your plan of overcoming any situation is not possible.

For instance, your faith in God to heal you is what makes you overcome sicknesses, diseases, and infirmities in your life. Your faith in God to provide for you is what makes you overcome adversity. So if you must overcome any crisis or situation in your life, you must have faith in God.

CHAPTER 10

CREATING A FUTURE FOR YOURSELF

*You don't wait for the future,
but you create the future.*
—Apostle Johnson Sulemane

After decades of horrible and unbearable experiences and challenges that I had to endure, I have been working tirelessly toward creating a future that will impact me, others in my surroundings, and the world at large positively.

Putting a smile on the faces of orphans, widows, war-affected and underdeveloped nations around the world, and taking young girls and young boys from the streets who have been abused by drugs, alcoholism, prostitution, and rape have been my focus.

The kind of future you will have depends to a large extent on the things that you do now. Whatever you desire for your future, you need to start working toward that now through prayers, education, and hard work. So stop waiting on the future and move toward creating for yourself a future in which you can impact the lives of others meaningfully while at the same time living comfortably. Years will go by, and you will not make any progress in life if you do not work toward it.

Hard work and creativity are the two cardinal things that can enable you to achieve your desired future. There is no future for a lazy man. The future is only for the hard workers. Many people desire a glorious future of living a life better than the one that they are currently living, but they are very lazy and, therefore, are finding it so difficult to accomplish their goal.

Do not only be hardworking in your endeavor to actualize your desired future, but you must add creativity to your hard work. This is because it is only when the forces of hard work and creativity have been demonstrated together by you that you can achieve the result you desire.

Remember, in the book of Genesis, it was by these two forces that God brought about the future that he desired for the human race on his throne one day. As God was sitting on his throne in heaven, He desired in His heart to create a future for humans, and His desire to create a future for humans became a reality without delay by the two cardinal forces of hard work and creativity.

In Genesis 1:1, the Bible says, "In the beginning, God created the heaven and the earth." How did God create heaven and the earth? God created heaven and earth by working seven days. Understand here that God was not just working, but God was working with the ability to create.

Creativity is the product of work, and the product of work, which is creativity, is the benefit of work. So work without creativity is work in vain. Whenever you are working toward creating a future for yourself, you must work with the ability to create opportunities that will enable you to attain your desired goal.

This is how it works. By working, you can utilize the creative ability that you inherited from God, your creator, and by utilizing your creative ability, you are able to create opportunities that can enable you to accomplish your desired future.

It is obvious that things can be difficult at the beginning of working toward the realization of your desired future. But never give up because the blessings that the future holds for you are not at the beginning, but they are at the end.

Never wait for big jobs and big money before you start working toward the accomplishment of your future goals. You can start working toward achieving your future with the little that you have now because it is from the little that God will do big things.

God does not use big things to do big things, but rather God uses small things to do big things. Never despise your humble beginnings, but it is your humble beginnings that God will use to give you a greater end (Zechariah 4:10).

CHAPTER 11

LESSONS LEARNED

It is important to forgive those who wrong you so that your prayers will not be hindered and you will have less stress. Just ask God to remove every hatred from your heart. As for those whom you may have wronged, and they don't want to listen to you, ask God to take the hatred out of their hearts.

Disappointments are inevitable so learn to rely on the Almighty God and yourself only. When they do occur, He will see you through; and because you are self-reliant, you will not be knocked off your feet.

We all experience shame and are vulnerable at some point in our lives. The more you think about what has occurred, the worse your pain becomes, and it is not good for your health. So you have to let go of the pain and anger.

Shame keeps you stuck because you are afraid of losing the little comfort you may have. So you prefer to continue holding on rather than moving forward. The thing is, no amount of shame will ever make you feel better.

Keep in mind that the way people treat you reflects who they are and in no way defines you. Don't let what others say about you stop you from pursuing your dreams. They are entitled to their opinions, but they are not God. Speak to God on your knees about your plans and trust Him without any doubt, and He will lift you up.

Life is worth living despite all the challenges. So at some point, you must accept what has happened as being part of life and move forward, always praying for God to strengthen you.

PRACTICAL LESSONS TO LEARN ABOUT MY GRANDMOTHER'S VILLAGE LIFE

While growing up as a child in the hands of my grandmother in the village and watching her live like a villager, I discovered some practical lessons about her village life that I would like to share with you in this chapter that I believe will motivate you.

She was old, yet she was strong and hardworking.

Many old people are retired and stop working when they reach the age of sixty and upward. The truth is that, despite your old age of sixty, seventy, or eighty, you can still work hard toward achieving your goals. Never allow the devil to remind you of your old age and use it to hinder you from working hard toward achieving your goals, as well as actualizing your dreams. If you were working in the government of your country or with a private institution and in subsequent time you were retired, because you reach the retirement age, don't go home, and sit down for the rest of your life. Instead, you should start an initiative like a company or a private business that will enable you to keep working.

Do not be complacent with the achievements that you have had from your previous job. Neither are you to rely on your retirement benefits and just sit home for the rest of your life without doing something meaningful and productive to enhance your worth and value to society.

My grandmother was a very old woman. Despite her old age, she still went to her farm and worked hard planting crops and harvesting them during the harvest season. You can also do the same thing. Never allow your age to create an atmosphere of gloominess and hopelessness, but rather keep working toward achieving your dreams as long as you have the strength.

If you want to be full of joy, enthusiasm, and laughter in your old age, then do not give up on what you may have failed to accomplish during your youthful days. Keep working toward achieving it. The fact that you did not achieve something that you may have desired when you were young does not, in any way, mean that you can't achieve it in your old age.

Her excellency Madam Ellen Johnson Sirleaf, the former president of the Republic of Liberia, started dreaming of the presidency when she was a teenager. Her dream was not fulfilled until she became an old woman. She kept hoping and working hard toward achieving her goal of becoming president until she succeeded as the twenty-fourth President of Liberia at the age of sixty-eight.

What you need to build your courage and confidence in working tirelessly toward achieving your goals in your old age is hope. If you have been dreaming of becoming a president or being a millionaire from your youthful days, you can still work toward actualizing your dream of becoming a president, even while in your old age. My grandmother was old, but despite her age, she never stopped working until the Lord called her home. This is a lesson that you can learn from her in this book.

She was uneducated, yet she was a woman of wisdom.

Wisdom is the ability to use your knowledge and experience to make good decisions and judgments. There is a difference between wisdom and knowledge from a biblical standpoint. Wisdom is the ability to discern or judge what is true, right, or lasting. Knowledge, on the other hand, is information gained through experience, reasoning, or acquaintance.

Knowledge can exist without wisdom but not the other way around. One can be knowledgeable without being wise. For instance, knowledge is knowing when to use a gun; wisdom knows when to keep it holstered. In other words, wisdom is the application of knowledge. You can acquire knowledge of something as much as you can, but it takes wisdom to use your acquired knowledge to your advantage.

That is, without the use of wisdom, you can never benefit adequately from the education you acquire in any specific field. Many around the globe are well educated, but they are not immensely benefiting from their education the way they should be because they lack wisdom. For instance, the wisdom of God demands that a person with numerous academic accomplishments be able to use their education in a way that will benefit others by opening up businesses in their field of study that will cause others to be employed instead of just sitting and waiting for the government.

Anyone who is educated to a higher level but still working under someone else to survive shows that the person lacks the wisdom of God. The truth is that if someone has the wisdom of God, he would know what to do to create employment for himself as well as for others. My grandmother was not educated, but she was a woman of wisdom. She never went to any university on earth to learn about farming, but by the wisdom of God, she knew how to go about her business of farming.

What is wisdom, and what is not wisdom?

Wisdom is not the product of schooling, but it is the product of life's experiences. Wisdom is not the act of arguing all day long, but it is the act of letting go before the sun can go down in order to overcome your anger and thereby set yourself free from the sin of resentment, bitterness, and unforgiveness.

Wisdom is not the gift of education, but it is a gift from God (James 1:5). Wisdom is not demonstrated by anxiety, but it is demonstrated by patience.

Wisdom can never intensify conflict, but it is a catalyst that can be used to resolve conflict.

ANGEL SCERE

*There was no pastor around the village to preach to
her about prayer, yet she was a woman of prayer.*

Prayer should be offered to God based on your relationship with Him and not based on the preaching of your pastor about prayer or based on your desire for something that you need from God. When you pray to God based on the motivational messages of your pastor, then it means that when you find yourself in a geographical location where your pastor or a man of God is not around to motivate you to pray, you will definitely not pray. When you pray to God based on your relationship with Him, whether a man or a woman of God is around to encourage you to pray or not, you will still call on the name of Jesus, that has the power to save you.

On the other hand, when your prayer is based on your desire for something you need from God, then it simply means that if you don't have a desire, you will not pray to God. When it is based on your relationship with God, you will always pray.

My grandmother was always prayerful because her prayer was not based on the encouragement of a pastor about prayer, nor was her prayer based on a desire for something that she needed from God. Her prayer was based on her relationship with God. This is a lesson that you can learn from my grandmother's village life in this book.

If you are proactive, you make things happen instead of waiting for them to happen to you. *Active* means "doing something." The prefix *pro* means "before." So if you are proactive, you are ready before something happens. The opposite is being reactive or waiting for things to unfold before responding.

Think about the winter season. A proactive person washes his hands and takes vitamins. A reactive person gets sick and takes cold medicine.

The word *slothful* means not easily aroused to activity. Lazy or slothful implies a temperamental inability to act promptly or speedily when action or speech is called for. There are reasons why you can still fulfill dreams in your old age that you failed to fulfill in your youthful age:

1. Despite you being an old man or woman, you still have the Holy Spirit living in you.
2. You are old physically, but you are not old mentally. Your five senses are still working.
3. The Bible says, in old age, you can still produce fruits.
4. Your old age may be the point at which God has a purpose to do what he promised to do in your life.
5. An overcomer is one who believes and is not a unbeliever.
6. An overcomer is one who is born again.

CHAPTER 12

MY ACHIEVEMENTS OVER THE YEARS

Angel, who did not go to school when she lived in the village and who could not go to English school when she was a refugee in Côte d'Ivoire because her grandmother had no money to send her, now holds the following academic achievements or diplomas:

- Rainbow Academy High School, Abidjan, Ivory Coast, West Africa
- Brookhaven Community College of Dallas, Texas, USA, as a pharmacy technician
- ITS Academy of Arlington, Texas, USA, in cosmetology

Angel now runs a non-profit organization called Angel Foundation (angelsfoundation.me), which she founded and currently serves as a CEO. It is located in Dallas, Texas, and caters to homeless victims, less-fortunate children, widows, single mothers, etc. The Angel Foundation assists people in war-affected communities and villages in underdeveloped nations with food and other items needed to sustain them.

Angel served as the first brand ambassador for *Sapphire Emerald Magazine* in New Jersey, United States of America.

Angel is an author, a motivational speaker, and a philanthropist who is passionate about putting smiles on the faces of orphans, less-fortunate kids, widows, etc.

She is a humanitarian, a philanthropist, and an advocate for young girls and boys involved with drug abuse, alcoholism, prostitution, etc. She is a motivational speaker who assists people in discovering their personal purpose and developing their true potential.

ABOUT THE AUTHOR

Angel Venus Scere is the founder and CEO of the Angel Foundation, a humanitarian organization organized and existing under the laws of the State of Texas, United States of America. This foundation helps homeless victims on the streets, provides food, and reaches out to orphans, less-fortunate children, widows, single mothers, etc., in communities and villages of war-affected and underdeveloped nations of the world.

She is a humanitarian, a philanthropist, and an advocate for young girls and boys dealing with drug abuse, alcoholism, prostitution, and so on. She is an international speaker who empowers people to discover their personal purpose and develop their true potential.

Angel is a graduate of the Rainbow Academy High School, Abidjan, Ivory Coast, West Africa, a graduate of Brookhaven Community College of Dallas, Texas, USA, as a pharmacy technician, and a graduate of the ITS Academy of Arlington, Texas, USA, with a diploma in cosmetology.

Angel is an author, a motivational speaker, and a philanthropist whose heartbeat is to put a smile on the faces of orphans, less-fortunate kids, widows, and so on.

CPSIA information can be obtained
at www.ICGtesting.com
Printed in the USA
LVHW040848280623
750900LV00002B/277